AF430070

don't need me.

don't need me. by Jamie Winters

for Heather

who isn't able to fight anymore.
I'm sorry we couldn't be there for you.
We love you.

and for Sayge

who is still fighting.
You are so loved. Please never give up.

a note to the readers.

The poems in this book are based off of serious conditions that can cause intense emotions. While I've tried to keep direct references out of poems, the emotions of the poems may still cause an emotional flare up if this is a sensitive subject for you. If at any time while reading this book you start having negative feelings that may be dangerous, please do not hesitate to reach out for help.

National Suicide Hotline: 1-800-273-TALK

Text BRAVE to 741741

Or chat: https://suicidepreventionlifeline.org/chat/

table of contents.

preface.

When I first published *i'm fine* in May 2018, I never had any intention of publishing another haiku collection similar to it. I was still writing haiku about my struggles with mental illness, of course. Haiku are one of the best ways I've found to quickly take an emotion, wrap it up and send it outside of my own head, without the pressure of working on a long project. But after I finished *i'm fine*, I didn't think I would have anything new and worthwhile to say. I wrote haiku for myself, but didn't think there would be any value for them outside of the act of writing.

Or at least, that was what I thought until I recently looked back over my files of poetry and began to realize just how much I've changed and grown in the two years since I released that first collection. And I began thinking that maybe I actually had something else to say, after all.

i'm fine is a story of grief, mainly the kind of grief that happens when our own lives don't turn out the way we planned. *don't need me* is a continuation of sorts, picking up from where *i'm fine* left off and delving more into what happens when you start picking up the pieces from the raw process of grief and start deciding where you're going to go next. It's about choosing to consciously grow and change into a better person, even though it hurts like hell. It's about learning how to know what you need and set boundaries rather than pretending—the difference between saying *i'm fine* versus *don't need me*.

For that reason, *don't need me* is arranged differently. Instead of being organized into sections based on the stages of grief, I chose to organize the sections of this collection based on the stages of alchemy, the process of transforming raw material into something valuable. Most people know of the alchemy of fiction and history where alchemists tried to turn lead into gold, but this book is based on emotional alchemy. While the stages are the same, emotional alchemy focuses on transforming the raw material of the soul and spirit, refining and purifying a person's essence until they are "gold," in a sense.

Other than that, the style choices between this collection and *i'm fine* are similar. The poems are still lowercase because that's how I write when my emotions get too strong. The haiku in this collection still break many of the traditional "rules" of haiku, and should technically be called senryu and not haiku at all. But they still helped me to find peace among the pain and chaos, and I think that gets at some of the true spirit of what haiku is meant to be.

I hope that if you liked *i'm fine* that this collection can add a new layer of depth to the original haiku I wrote. And whether you have or haven't read *i'm fine*, then I hope these poems can help to put some difficult emotions into words and remind you that you are never alone.

Calcination

to burn.

panic bubbling
barely underneath my skin—
shush. have a soda.

i'm just so tired
but I'm terrified of sleep
paralyzed awake

hiding in fear from
the scary conversations
of obligation

we still aren't safe yet
how do i keep myself sane
when life's uncertain?

always sitting there
stress in the back of my mind
never leaving me

what if i say things
that turn people against me
though I didn't know?

i don't want to stress
but that's the only way things
will ever get done

waking in a sweat
i don't know what i can do
to fix up my life

tears aren't coming out
i feel them pool in my heart
and i am flooded

panic like a string
humming and shaking in me
because it got plucked

i want out right now
all I can feel is panic
swirling tornado

i can't concentrate
on the things i need to do
through this haze of fear

why won't it just stop?
all i want is this to stop
please stop, just stop, stop

watch me burn it up
everyone i love gets burned
a pyro at life

corners of eyes hurt
at all the forgotten pains
of this long lifetime

there are so many
i'll never find an escape—
monsters of my mind

do you still see me?
or have i faded away,
a dusty relic?

guilt is a boulder
crushing out of my lungs
when i remember

every word hurting
pulled slowly from a heartstring
not wanting to leave

i want to be me
but i feel myself slipping
until i'm no one

try to rip off this
invisibility cloak—
write poems to myself

somehow you're gone now
and i don't know how to cope
but life still goes on

missing memories
scattered through my mind like weeds
leaving behind holes

i keep turning around
only to find empty space
where my life should be

to melt.

something needs to change
i'm tired of being stuck
i want life to start

the cat understands
my pain better than i do
deep, unblinking eyes

i want to go home
except i'm already home
but this isn't home

do i have a goal?
is there something to reach for?
or is this pointless?

This life is stupid
but it's still all that i've got—
still want something else

i want a rescue
like i dreamed of as a teen
discontent remains

stretching through the room
a lonely ray of starlight
reminds me to dream

tell me something new
give me hope i can cling to
when mine has run out

i wish i knew what
would break through my bad training
and fix everything

i want to be strong
but building strength takes so much
pain tolerance

i wish i could be
reckless like i once was
so very long ago

i just want someone
to tell me it's all okay
and i believe them

let me run away
let me become someone else
let this be easy

waiting for daybreak
it wriggles in my fingers
cling to scraps of hope

i don't think i am
as beautiful as you claim
i just can't be that

i have to give in
every piece of me eaten—
all consuming love

if only i could
be the person i know
underneath the stress

i need more cuddles
to ease the heartache and pain
i can always feel

i just want to rest
from all of my worrying
focus on living

growing stronger yet
until i have new armor
made from this new hope

to split.

want to run away,
but can't make my body move
my soul divided

i'm just so tired
always fighting to exist
never existing

still struggling with
how to make my heart feel whole
after years of pain

help me run away
but you want me to fight this
you should fight instead

don't tell me it's fine
when absolutely nothing
will be fine again

why am i like this?
why can't i just be stronger?
why do i fall down?

why do you admire
the person i was back then
when i've changed so much?

why do you admire
the person i've become now
when i'm still so flawed?

this isn't my face
it follows me everywhere
haunted by myself

i wish i could run
away from the me i hate
run till it's better

i don't want to try
i don't want to keep pushing
i don't want this life

this is not my life
but i still have to pretend
that this is all mine

guess i'll fight your war
while you sit on the sidelines
shaded from the blood

what is left to do?
what else haven't i tried yet?
what's left to save me?

i feel dangerous
you should stay away from me—
i should stay away

warm ball of anger
settled deep in my stomach
as my voice rises

why won't you give up?
what will it take to end this?
why are you still here?

don't even pretend
as if you care about me
when even i don't

i no longer know
if i'm really as strong as
people say i am

i need to just stop
walk away from this habit
you aren't serving me

i wish we'd never
ended things the way we had
what other way was there?

my words don't comfort—
she wanders the house, crying
who knows why she's sad?

i understand why
this pain is known as heartbreak
because I feel torn

i'd like to tell you
but I don't know who i am
except mistaken

Conjunction to marry.

if only I knew
the anxious thoughts you're thinking
so much like my own

i feel stretched too thin
there isn't enough of me
to cover it all

my soul is tired
but I have to find a way
to keep pushing through

i still have to fight
even when i want to faint
can't have luxury

things will change soon, right?
i don't know how long i can
keep surviving this

i can't measure up
to who i once thought i was
when i was younger

i don't seem to grow
because i'm still in this place
when you all moved on

i'm scared for the day
you finally realize
i will let you down

i'm sorry i suck
at pretty much everything
that seems worth doing

i want to write more
but it feels like words are stuck
on fragments of pain

i need ideas
bashing my head against walls
wishing for insight

when my tears get stuck
two kneading paws come find me
to coax my grief out

remind me of peace
even though things are so hard
i want to go on

sometimes roars are mews,
but a tiger's a tiger
roars will come someday

Fermentation to putrefy.

i am overgrown
vines wrapping around my heart
and squeezing tighter

what is left to gain
from pushing myself like this?
i want to give up

my brain is fuzzy
with all the things i need to do
and still can't manage

blankets calling me
to crawl into their soft cave
and just disappear

my heart's still broken
life moves around me in waves
i stand there, still stunned

i need to get up
i need to move forward now
i'm still sitting here

so much to be done—
sitting shocked, wrapped in blankets
staring at the wall

where is the magic
that i once saw everywhere
why has it left me?

crying without tears
no one around even knows
my world is breaking

watch life tick away
while praying i don't mess up
if i haven't yet

wishing for my bed
i feel i've hardly been up
then i sleep again

it's easier to
give up on all of my dreams
than failing myself

blanket of blue stars
hides me away from the world
the stars in neat rows

neither here nor there
the static on a tv
i've misplaced myself

voice inside my ear
whispering that no one cares
i can't shake it off

so many people
have cut me out of their lives
and i didn't notice

forget about me
there's nothing left worth saving
go find someone else

i don't want to try
so why won't i let myself
give up already?

these aren't pretty poems
about finding hope and light—
can't write something else

grimace through seasons
feeling time slipping away
unsure what to do

i just want to sleep
without waking up until
these problems are fixed

looking for the light
when these dark nights are so long
remembering's hard

still so much to do
the list is never ending—
i'll never get out

i'm tired and cold
and i want today to leave,
forget it happened

singing "this job sucks!"
doesn't stop the sucking much
or make it better

nothing's good enough
through these bitter eyes of mine
still keep creating

another haiku
i don't have words worth saying
i'm just so tired

when i feel darkest
i hear wisdom of a sage
know that i am loved

Distillation
to purify.

when night is darkest
i feel fur brush my fingers
invisible purrs

still feeling echoes
of a pain that won't leave me
i have to trudge on

at least it's echoes
instead of the gaping void
i was yesterday

eyelids so heavy
still i force myself awake
in obligation

i've pushed for so long
i feel like i don't exist
all i am is will

still moving forward
even when kicked in the heart—
getting up again

i don't have control
over almost anything
but i can still write

brain spinning around
caught in a merry-go-round
in a sea of fog

just keep on trekking
the path is always uphill
but keep on trekking

paper is infinite—
stretching up to the heavens
then small and fragile

sweet and smooth velvet
keeping the demons at bay
for just one more night

life moves so slowly
except when it moves quickly
why can't i choose when?

she cried the whole way
even wanted change is hard
when trapped in a cage

do you know this man?
but the mirror doesn't say
never speaks to me

to succumb.

i realize now
i need a little more faith
i need to believe

try to concentrate
on something other than fear—
remember hope's flame

knots in my stomach
learning to trust is so hard
but so important

the same teeth that kill
can also pick up kittens
gentle as can be

i thought i wanted—
but none of that matters now
what i want is love

guess who's still standing?
well, i may have fallen down
but i'm still alive

i still can't believe
the things i have accomplished—
but never alone

not all of my life
is made to revolve around
productivity

i found this myself
even though it's small and weak
i fought for this strength

i give willingly
not because of what i'll gain—
or i wouldn't gain

don't think of the end—
take comfort in the journey
you're still on your way

you are here to sing—
when you feel your voice cracking
you must keep singing

we are built from love
despite the hate thrown out way
we build from the good

i renounce my will
i know i can't know what's right
in my tiny world

my art teacher said,
"start with a line of movement"
always start with life

courage to exist
is not won so easily
it takes a lifetime

standing on my legs
with hardly any strength left
but it's all my own

i'm doing my best
i'll be where i need to be
i wholly trust you

i feel so relieved—
how good to be a human,
to make bold mistakes

i become ashes
in the fire of mental health
then grow from myself

thank you.

Thank you so much for reading *don't need me*. I hope you enjoyed the book!

If you enjoy my poetry, I have seven other poetry books out, including *i'm fine*, my first mental health haiku collection. And I always have more poetry collections coming out! If you'd like to keep up with my new releases, you can join my mailing list at http://eepurl.com/dwWXoH. I only use email to communicate about book news, promise.

And if you have a moment, please consider leaving a review at Amazon or Goodreads. As an author, I love looking through reviews to see what my readers have enjoyed and what I could improve on. And as a reader, I love looking to reviews for advice when I'm trying to find a new book to enjoy. Reviews are a great way to help keep our book community connected!

Thanks again for reading, and I hope to see you around again in the future!

Jamie Winters

notes on alchemy.

When going through the process of spiritual alchemy, it doesn't always happen in a straightforward manner. You may go through one stage and end up having to go back and do another stage all over again, sort of like sifting a stubborn batch of flour. And within one stage, you may experience glimpses of other stages. You could even find all the stages contained within one phase, like a fractal. This is part of why I was able to have a somewhat even distribution of poems through the stages.

Of course, fermentation was still the largest of the sections, and that's because this is the phase I have been in recently. Being in it currently has led to more poems being written about it. If you are curious, here is a basic guide to what each stage can mean emotionally and what I was using to help me figure out where to place poems. I mostly based my decisions and understanding of the stages from the explanations in the book *On Becoming an Alchemist: A Guide for the Modern Magician* by Catherine MacCoun. If you're intrigued by the concept of emotional alchemy, I highly recommend you check it out.

Calcination: To burn
The breaking down of ego, self-doubt, stubbornness, self-sabotaging, pride, and arrogance. Destroying that which is excess, not us, learning what we are not, and making room for new growth.

Dissolution: To melt

Less identification with our false self. We become aware we're affecting others. Learning to exist in a state of desire that makes us reach upwards and causes disappointment at not getting what we long for.

Separation: To split

Becoming aware of our authentic feelings. Separating what our thoughts, feelings, and self are versus what we are not. Creating boundaries to better fill our own potential. The difference between high and low, inner and outer.

Conjunction: To marry

A time of introspection and solitude. Recombining the purified parts of ourselves. Our two sides may not agree, but both are necessary, both good, both understood.

Fermentation: To putrefy

Death of the old self. The dark night of the soul. Feeling hopeless about our progress and everything we experienced before feels crazy and made up. A reluctance to express ourselves and loss of initiative.

Distillation: To purify

Integration of the things we've learned into daily life. Purifying what we've learned into something usable. The powerful magician whose magic is untamed and a little out of control. A disconnection between intention and will.

Coagulation: To succumb

Breaking free. To get a glimpse of god's will; god and magician meet. A sudden onset of humility and realizing how small and non powerful the magician actually is in reality. Sometimes the only way to use magic is to tell it, "Magic, do as you will."

about the author.

Jamie Winters has been struggling with mental illness for most of his life. When medicine and therapy have struggled to help, writing has been there as an additional lifeline. Jamie is still struggling with mental illness, but believes there is good in sharing the journey with others even when still caught in the storm. He makes a point of trying to talk openly about his own mental illness in the hopes of one day being a guiding light for someone else.

If you would like to keep up with Jamie Winters' journey, you can follow him online at jamiewintersauthor.wordpress.com

also by Jamie Winters.

i'm fine.
A Haiku Collection About Mental Illness

words can't describe this
feeling of bricks on my heart
so i say "i'm fine."

https://mybook.to/imfine

TransVerse
Poetry About Being Transgender

Before you come,
You ought to know
The name I use
Isn't the name I'm called
At home

https://mybook.to/transversepoetry

Neko Haiku
Poetry for Cat Lovers

How could I better
Catch a cat's fleeting beauty
Than in a haiku?

https://mybook.to/nekohaiku

Ink Wisteria
Poems About Writing

I find myself wistful
for when the words came easily,
when every day was filled with
ink splattered notebooks and the clickety clack of
keys.

https://mybook.to/inkwisteria